BANISHING THE BOOGIEMAN

Parents Survival Guide:
Helping Your Children Through Nighttime Fear

by Lucia Davindia Steele

This book is dedicated to my three children…
Two that have come through me
and one who has come to me.
I love you all.

TABLE OF CONTENTS

ACKNOWLEDGMENTS

Thanks to God for my strength and for leading me to my husband Cameron who is my rock, my support, my best friend and the one who keeps encouraging me to face my fears. Thanks to my children for making me a better person even when it looks like at times I'm the opposite. Thanks to my fears for showing me that there is more to life than what meets the eye. Thanks to my Mom & Dad who tried their best and loved me to pieces. To my sister and brother who left me downstairs to turn the lights off after the movie *Fantasm* - you guys suck! Thanks to my friend, soul sister and much needed voice of reason and inspiration Jovanna Joan Casey, your perspectives and knowledge are invaluable. Thanks to my many teachers: Zara Angel, Eric Dowsett, Brenda Miller, Christopher Howard, Gary Craft, JoAnne Rohn Cook, Richard Sutphen, Eldon Taylor, Cecilia Schukar, Dr. Daniel Amen, Dr. Billie Sahley, Howard Glassner and all of the authors and guests that help me learn and grow in a loving way. And Thank You to all the momma's I've talked with, shared with in frustration and joy in moving our little ones to courage, understanding and self-trust.

Disclaimer: *Unless otherwise indicated, information in this book is based on research and opinions formulated by Lucia Davindia Steele. Ms. Steele is not a doctor nor claims to be one. The tools outlined in this book are not proven to cure medical conditions. It is always recommended that you consult with your doctor, psychologist or therapist before applying these techniques.*

INTRODUCTION

"Fear is a tool used for navigating life,
not directing it."
~Lucia Davindia Steele~

Parents, be warned, this is not a book on child behavior. This is a guide to help you not only liberate your child from nighttime fears, but ultimately, through your guidance, empower them into self-trust and self-reliance.

Now let me clarify. There are times when it is imperative to take precaution using fear as your gauge. Fear is a primal, guttural response to danger. To discount that emotional response can be extremely dangerous, even life threatening. But when fear becomes a way of living, it stunts us tremendously in ways we never would imagine.

If you are a parent or caregiver of one, ten or twenty children, you know firsthand how little time there is to read a book cover to cover. And I'm sure you've already tried a number of things that haven't worked and you're looking for more clues to help your child, therefore, I've intentionally made this book brief and to the point so you have some tools to work with immediately. I'm proud to say that you can be partially brain dead from being up all night with your little one and still get something out of this book. If you just don't have the time to read this book from cover to cover, feel free to go straight to Chapter 10.

Throughout this book I will share some anecdotal stories to illustrate points made throughout this guide, but I will keep that to a minimum as we want to help your child sooner than later.

My inspiration to write this book has many layers. First and foremost are my own kids, Jadon and Phoenix. Both of my sons have, at one point or another, experienced night terrors, sleep walking, "monsters" and "ghosts" that keep them up and feeling vulnerable. I can empathize, because as a kid, I too had some of those same experiences.

Another reason I am writing this book… many parents have been asking me for resources to help them with their children who have their own "boogiemen" to deal with and don't know how to handle it. I've yet to find one book that really resonated with me, my experiences and gave step by step tools to alleviate the challenges we as parents face… I figured, I'd write my own perspectives since I've had so much success with my children and other children in helping them "banish their boogieman".

What qualifies me as an "expert"?

Well first and foremost, I am a mother who has had great success in helping my children move through their fears. I have been trained in regression therapy, dowsing and vibrational healing. I am also an expert in the field of innovation. My husband Cameron and I co-hosted a radio program together for eight years interviewing pioneering speakers on cutting edge healing technologies and modalities. It has been a grand expansion of knowledge researching and speaking to leading doctors, therapists, physicists and spiritual workers over the years.

We have since evolved our program into an international radio station. I now divide my time overseeing the operation of our station, writing, mentoring many individuals with my husband in intimate relationship building and parental guidance and most importantly of all... I am "Wife" and "Mommy".

I only want to be of service to others, and hopefully impart some helpful tools and information that will ease your child's fears.

I do want to mention, there is a point with all of this, whether your child is 3, 8, 13 or 18 that you may need to consult your physician as there may be a physiological symptom to something else. Use your gut to determine this. Only you know your child the best.

So let's start helping your little one.

CHAPTER 1

Okay Night... What's the Deal?

"Each time we face our fear, we gain strength,
courage, and confidence in the doing."
~Anonymous~

As a parent you've probably looked under your kid's bed or in their closet plenty of times, only to your child's relief and dismay, to find nothing there.

Then what is it? What is your kid so afraid of, and why is it only happening at night?

Is little Johnny afraid of the dark? Not necessarily.

It could be a number of rational things with a rational explanation. Or it could be one really freaky thing that scares the "you-know-what" out of most people. But we won't go there... yet.

So why is Johnny playing out his anxieties at night? What's been going on for him? What is he exposed to that is short circuiting his system?

Let's take a look at darkness for a minute.

The safety and security of the womb is dark. Seeds sprout to create beautiful flowers or ripe vegetables underground in the dark.

Has the power in your home ever gone out, and you have to go to the basement to reset the breaker box and gotten the willies? Or in the middle of the night hear water running only to realize that one of the kids left the hose on outside, and you have to go turn it off and feel like you have to look around five times? If you can relate... there is a remnant of fear that creeps in and potentially throws you off balance. And you only feel this way when it's night!

Now think of your level of discomfort in those moments. And imagine how that anxiety compounds in a little body that doesn't have the knowledge and reference points you have as an adult.

But what knowledge are we talking about? We'll get to that.

In the dark, we lose much of our sense of sight. Therefore, our other senses (i.e. sound, smell, taste, touch) have to pick up the slack, if we are not used to paying attention to those other senses we can become anxious and unsure of ourselves and our surroundings. That anxiety and uncertainty simply perpetuates fear.

In little Johnny's room, when the lights are out, his senses are heightened. Depending on what he has been exposed to and his imagination, daddy walking down the hall could be the steps of a monster. Or a shadow cast by a hallway light, street light or night light could be a ghost.

Fear is a healthy response to feeling physically or emotionally unsafe. We use fear to make positive decisions for ourselves. Don't walk down that alley. Keep your distance from wild animals. Don't go swimming at the top of a waterfall. You know... little things like that.

We teach our kids early not to talk to strangers, because they could be taken away... not to run in the middle of the street because they can get hit by a car... not to pet animals we don't know because they might get bitten. These statements are all true to a degree. And I'm sorry to say, and to disagree with a popular parenting belief, little ones need a **_little bit_** of fear to "respect" the rules.

But when we start using fear to run our lives... such as, "I'm not going to ride a bike because I'm afraid I will fall."... "I'm not going to learn how to swim because I'm afraid of water."... It can snowball into a pattern of missed opportunities such as, "I'm not going to apply for that job, because I'm afraid I'm not good enough."... "I'm not going to ask that person out, because I'm afraid of being rejected."... You get my point.

Little Johnny is at his most tender time right now. He is moving from imagination to reality back to imagination. What is real? What can be said or proven to Johnny that will help ease his fear?

There are theories that we are hardwired to be afraid of the dark. All humans, at one point in our history, were prey to predatory animals. It is still the case for indigenous tribes everywhere in the world. The individuals who live with those areas of danger are aware and take the appropriate precautions. You see it on National Geographic, Discovery and Animal Planet. So no matter how far away from your reality it may be, it's still in our collective conscience. From my perspective, night time fear is very real and justifiable.

I have to admit, when I go outside, I keep my eyes peeled for raccoons. In Alaska it may be a bear or cougar. In areas of Florida, it could be an alligator. There are some things in the dark that we really need to be conscientious of.

Does your little one talk about a fear of animals or being vulnerable to physical harm?

The other theory is that we are taught to be afraid of the dark. We're taught through stories, movies and most of all, our imagination of the unknown. I don't know about you, but _I_ had anxiety the first time Bruce the shark from _Finding Nemo_ came up on the movie screen. And I was with my four year old at the time.

I was raised in a home where my mother loved watching scary movies, and my dad told great ghost stories. I can picture my dad now with a flashlight under his chin in his deep theatrical voice, "Once upon a tiiimmme!". We would all squeal and wiggle in our seats, or cling to my mom.

Bottom line, as fun as that was, and the great memories I have from it - it's scared the poop out of me at five years old.

Do you remember enjoying being scared? Maybe you still do. But for our kids, there needs to be a balance that brings them back to safety. Our kids have to know that unequivocally mommy and daddy are here to make sure they are safe, and that they can and will be able to make themselves safe too.

One of our jobs as parents is to help them gain courage, and trust their instincts; that may be through your faith or values. Either way, children require something positive and meaningful they can anchor to, giving them a touchstone for self-confidence and self-trust. It will be one of the most important lessons we teach them and that they will ever learn.

And it all starts with knowledge.

CHAPTER 2

The Anatomy of a Fear Riddled Youth

"You have to know who you are,
if you don't you'll have nightmares."
~Stephen Rea~

Hello. My name is Lucia Davindia Steele and I was a fear riddled youth.

I have to put some levity around this because fear is a scary business. Especially when you're little one is involved.

I find my fears still surface a bit when one of my kids tell me something went "bump in the night" or they thought they saw something. Even though I have, over the years, worked to educate myself on what scares me, I still get that twinge reminding me of what my guys are going through, and I can assist them with compassion.

I'm going to share with you a "story" to help you understand how fear, if not adequately addressed, can imprint on your child and affect them in ways we may not expect, even well into adulthood.

Now bear with me, this is my journey as a child with fear. I do have a point with this chapter and it's not just to be narcissistic. You may be able to relate, or you may not. The purpose of this chapter is only to demonstrate the effects of dismissed and discounted emotions.

My entire life (up to 12 years ago) was propelled by inexplicable and unfounded fear. I simply felt unsafe. My parents did all they knew to make sure we lived in a good neighborhood, with good schools and encouraged us to be friends with "good" responsible people, but I was overwhelmed with fear… fear of the dark… fear of someone watching me… fear of someone physically hurting me… fear of someone emotionally hurting me… fear of not being loved. Simply put, I was immobilized by my fear.

Why?

My parents loved me and did all they knew to demonstrate that. So what could have happened to make me feel so unsure of life?

My answer… I didn't know how to trust myself…

As a very small child I remember feeling like I was being watched. I swore there was someone in my closet, under my bed, or just outside my bedroom door or window. I saw three shadows following me all the time. My parents did what most parents will, they told me that, "there wasn't anything to be afraid of." They opened my closet;

walked to the shadows; looked under the bed, and told me that nothing was there.

But I could still "feel" or "see" *something*.

As I mentioned earlier, my mom loved watching ghost stories. She still does to this day. This would prompt conversations between my parents on paranormal concepts. They would discuss their parents being "psychic". Movies and TV shows like Alfred Hitchcock, Twilight Zone, Unsolved Mysteries seemed to always be playing (aside from my mom's soap operas). If mom and dad were interested in what can't be explained, then there *had* to be a ghost in my closet!

But they kept saying there wasn't. So what was I to believe? What were the shadows? What was I feeling?

They didn't have any explanations, and this went on for a couple of years.

As I got slightly older and continued talking about my fears, my parents weren't quite as compassionate… they would get irritated and dismiss me. Finally I stopped telling my parents how scared I was, because their anger and irritation would affect me and make me, feel even more vulnerable. As my parents discounted my feelings, do did I. I started to not believe myself, and thought I was just being a coward and just plain stupid.

This started a life of doubting my feelings and my judgment.

"Other people are 'right'. Not me."

"My feelings don't count"

"I'm stupid."

"There's something wrong with me."

"Nobody understands me."

"If I say what's on my mind, people will get angry."

"If I say what's on my mind, no one will love me."

"Why am I so different?"

"Why am I so emotional?"

"Why am I so scared?"

So now, I was not only afraid of what my parents told me wasn't there. Rational or not, I was now afraid of losing their love and affection. I was afraid of being different. I was afraid of being strange. And I began to believe that my thoughts were wrong.

If I'm wrong, who am I? Can I trust my own conclusion in any matter?

Because I was operating from fear and self-doubt, I spent most of my life doing exactly what I was told (with minor expected rebellions here and there). I based my actions on my parents' experiences. Even though I had thoughts that were contrary to their beliefs; to stay "safe" and loved, I would follow the rules and ignore my feelings.

Not all kids will follow this model. This was my gig.

I was so stunted emotionally that I refused to have a boyfriend until my early 20's. Not because there were any parental restrictions, now older my new boogieman was called "intimacy". I projected fears of being rejected, and discounted by my parents on to any potential suitor. So I never really let anyone get too close. I was living all the clichés of "what not to do" in a relationship. I was just to "scared" to let another person know my feelings, because I was certain I would be rejected.

I began to have very short lived relationships. I was needy and clingy and just a hot mess. The fear of not being lovable pushed away any chance of a lasting relationship.

I was having constant mood swings and yes… I still felt like someone was watching me. By now, it was something I just ignored.

I was realizing that I was getting older, and the one thing I did want to experience was being married and having children. My fear wasn't strong enough to keep me from that goal… so I started looking at my fears, and understanding what drove me into my emotional paralysis.

At 23 I began my quest for deeper meaning and purpose. That quest, lead me on the path of love, compassion and humanity. I began anchoring myself in my relationship with my Maker, and found that my fears started to slightly dissipate.

When I met my husband and had my first son. All my fears and neurosis started resurfacing. I was "seeing" things again. I was still experiencing emotional mood swings. I had to figure out what I was so afraid of, and whether or not I was going crazy. I went to councilors and therapists that were helpful in making little leaps of progress, just not enough to make a difference.

I also met with my physician to have a hormone panel completed. My serotonin and dopamine levels were low. My estrogen and progesterone were all off kilter. My thyroid was working too slow and my adrenals were clinically fatigued.

I solved my problem! I know why I am so emotional, get anxious and have mood swings! Woohoo! I figured it out! So, I went on hormone replacement regimen, and felt even worse. I pressed on and had to investigate further.

What came first? Having adrenals out of whack, or female hormone issues?

Looking at adrenal fatigue for a moment. The hypothalamus, the pituitary gland, thyroid gland and adrenals are one of the main producers of hormones in our bodies. (Adrenals are the little gland that sit on top of your kidneys that produce cortisol.). Cortisol is the hormone that is released in response to stress.

Hmm. Fear causes stress.

When excessive amounts of cortisol is released, it results in significant physiological changes. Because I had spent so many years wired in fear, my adrenal glands were working overtime. So the adrenals had a direct effect on diminishing the production of other hormones.

So now I have a symptom of an issue… not the cause.

My ability to cope with stress was becoming less and less manageable. The emotions had taken their toll.

All this because of fear? Yeah, all this because of fear.

As I mentioned in the introduction, my husband and I hosted a radio talk show. Our process for selecting guests to interview arose from our life experiences, and personal growth interests.

We focused on specialists and authorities in various fields ranging from doctors, therapists, energy practitioners, hypnotherapists, philosophers, spiritual leaders… and the topic was always the same, anything and everything to do with self-improvement. The information from each professional we interviewed lent to the other giving me the tools to look at my shadows, and my light, helping me to move beyond my fears.

The biggest lesson I learned was from a word called "empathy" and a derivative of that word – "empathic".

When I discovered that I was a "sensitive empathic", it gave an answer to the "why". Why am I so different. Why am I so moody. Why am I so sensitive. I sat with the information and just cried. It made so much sense; even more than my hormonal train wreck.

I dove in head first to understand what empathy meant to me beyond the standard definition from the Merriam Webster dictionary, and how physical vibrations and frequencies impact a body. What am I feeling? What does it feel like? Is it my feeling, or am I "empathing" someone or something else?

All that to get to empathy? Yes.

CHAPTER 3

Is Your Child Empathic?

"The great gift of human beings is
that we have the power of empathy."
~Meryl Streep~

Merriam Webster's definition of empathy is:

1: the imaginative projection of a subjective state into an object so that the object appears to be infused with it.

2: the action of understanding, being aware of, being sensitive to, and vicariously experiencing the feelings, thoughts, and experience of another of either the past or present without having the feelings, thoughts, and experience fully communicated in an objectively explicit manner.

Number one deals with an imaginative projection. Number two is much more aligned to the empathic person. Both can be the case. In this chapter we will be focusing more on the second definition. Carl Jung originally coined the expression "innate sensitiveness" referring to a person who exhibited psychological sensitivity. Elaine N. Aron, Ph.d. explained these individuals as "highly sensitive" and goes into much detail in her book, *The Highly Sensitive Child*. She states that *"highly sensitive individuals are those born with a tendency to notice more in their environment and more deeply."*

A child begins to exhibit signs of empathy around 13 to 14 months of age. That does not necessarily mean they don't feel it before then. It means that their actions show that the child understands how to comfort a person who may be in emotional, or physical distress by that age. Empathy can be seen in newborns who begin to cry when another baby cries.

Everyone has empathy. Some people have their empathy meter amped up to full throttle, and others are on a very low governing system. Some are better at demonstrating empathy than others. The empathic person can pick up even the smallest change in environment (usually subconsciously). Anything from temperature change to an object that's been moved, or if mom, dad, sister, care provider or even pet had a stressful day. One of the best analogies for empathy is described by Catherine Crawford, author of *The Highly Intuitive Child*. She states *"If you take a tuning fork, strike it, and then place another tuning fork of similar size next to it without having them touch, the unstruck tuning fork will vibrate with the other one."* *Scientists call this "sympathetic resonance".* That is truly the case for the empathic child.

Here is a list of how to spot the empathic child:

- Sensitive to others in general.
- Sensitive to others emotions.
- Deeply understanding the feelings of others'.
- Challenged to identify the source of their emotions.
- Can't substantiate their feelings.
- Struggle or inability to distinguish one's feelings from another individual.
- Seems to know that there is more to what is said or seen.
- Difficulty in crowds.

Here are some examples of little ones demonstrating empathy –

Joey

Momma Jane has folded clothes and starts to put them away. Three and a half year old little Joey is watching her going back and forth in the house. Momma Jane is silently at work, but is preoccupied. She's been thinking about the conversation she had with her boss the other day, and is beginning to feel agitated.

Joey runs over to his mother and hugs her around the leg and says:

Joey: "I love you mommy. Are you mad?"

Jane: "I love you too honey. Why would you think I'm mad?"

Joey: "Are you happy?

Jane: "Yes, I'm happy."

(Remember she was agitated just when Joey stopped to ask her a question.) This little guy could sense his mothers tension. His mother naturally says yes she happy not to concern her child, but a three and a half year old picked up on her feelings of agitation.

Samantha

On a lazy Sunday afternoon, six year old Samantha is watching her favorite cartoon on the television. Her father Tom took the opportunity to have a little cat nap on the couch in the same room.

While Tom was sleeping, Samantha placed a blanket on him and began tucking him in.

Samantha is demonstrating care, and extending comfort to her father.

Eileen

Four year old Eileen was with her mother in the store searching for the nearest restroom. When Eileen's mother spotted the sign she pointed to it saying, "There it is!" Eileen ran full speed bumping into a smaller child going the opposite direction, knocking the child squarely to the ground.

The child she knocked down began to cry. Eileen was initially shocked by the collision, but when she paused and saw the little boy crying, Eileen's face turned red and eyes began to well up with tears.

Asking Eileen later why she started crying, she replied. "I felt really bad and it made me feel sad"

Ben

Five year old Ben went to the mall with his dad Harry. They walk into an electronics store that exhibited a large display that garnered a big crowd.

Little Ben almost immediately goes into a daze. He starts to wander away from his dad. Dad Harry has to pay extra close attention to Ben, because Ben is shutting down due to being overwhelmed by the chaos.

These are just a few example of how are kids demonstrate empathy in their environment.

Not every child will respond the same... but there is a noticeable change in behavior. I will quickly use my kids to show you a couple of different behaviors for empathic people in crowds.

My daughter Tia gets agitated and wants to withdraw in large groups. Both of my sons on the other hand get wired and out of control when they are in crowds.

It's also important to understand that highly empathic individuals aren't just sensitive to people, they are sensitive to places and things as well.

As I mentioned earlier, deeply empathic people have a built-in radar for subtle environmental changes.

But what kind of environmental changes are we really talking about?

CHAPTER 4

What Could it be and
Why is it Under My Bed?

"Human cells, far from being merely functional vessels, are in actuality electromagnetic fields of possibility and potential."
~Sol Luckman~

Think about the analogy of the tuning fork used in chapter three. It demonstrates how our bodies are finely tuned organisms that pick up on subtle vibrations. We are conductors for energy sending out a frequency. Even a rock has a physically measurable vibration with its own unique frequency.

Quartz crystals, a mineral, are used in clocks, computer mother-boards because of their electro-magnetic properties. The magnetic pulse of the earth is measured at about 7.8 Hertz. The human brain ranges from 0.5 Hertz to 30 Hertz.

If everything has a frequency and its own field of frequency, then we are connecting into multiple frequencies <u>at all times</u>.

You may have heard in the news the damage EMFs (electromagnetic field) can cause on the human body. EMFs can be created naturally or by electronic machinery.

Physicists define EMF as a "physical field produced by electrically charged objects."

Life forms have what is called "bio-electromagnatism". When our frequency is meshed with an EMF, it impacts our biological messaging systems throughout our body creating an internal communication breakdown.

A clinical and biological study was conducted between May 2008 and March 2010 by Professor Dominique Belpomme, a Clinical Oncologist at University Paris- Descartes.

"Of the 425 patients reporting hypersensitivity to electromagnetic fields (EMFs) were examined in a clinical and biological setting. Ninety-five percent of them clearly report the repeated occurrence and disappearance of symptoms linked to the presence or absence of EMFs. Three clinical phases were distinguished:

An initial stage during which EMF exposure can induce headaches, a sensation of heating in the ear and other parts of the body, especially the upper part of the body, tinnitus, ocular abnormalities. Myalgia, and in some cases, dermatitis and symptoms such as chest tightness, palpitations, tachycardia and nausea.

A second phase is characterized by insomnia, chronic fatigue and depressive tendencies, attention deficit, troubles with concentration, immediate memory loss, behavioral problems, and anxiety, during which the initial symptoms may occur every time the patient is exposed to EMF sources.

The third phase, suggests that an EMF intolerance syndrome may correspond to a pre-Alzheimer's disease state."

This same study shows there is a proven link between electromagnetic fields, cancer and leukemia.

In addition to headaches, depression and anxiety, other studies have reported that individuals exposed to EMFs have experienced anything from paranoia, suicide and nausea to loss of libido.

Now let's think of the deeply empathic person or highly sensitive person, and the effects that EMFs may have. What is your child really sensing? What are they really seeing? What are they really feeling?

I want to stress that the just because the federal government states that a certain level of EMFs, microwaves, radiation, etc. are "safe", doesn't mean it's true.

I briefly mentioned in chapter two that I began researching how vibration and frequency affected the body. A teacher by the name of Eric Dowsett was spotlighted on my radio show, and through his teachings, I learned how to physically identify energy fields using my empathic nature and heightened sensitivity to energy. Anyone can learn how to do this.

Eric put us through so many exercises and examples that it made understanding frequency in a palpable way. For example, as I mentioned, the earth has a frequency, and it emits various frequencies for a variety of naturally occurring geological reasons. Like underground water, major or minor fault lines and the like.

When stepping into the waves of these natural emitting frequencies you can *feel it*. Some may experience it as nausea, while still others may feel agitated or tired. Others may be energized.

I remember walking over a naturally occurring water way and immediately feeling nauseated, then stepping out and feeling normal. These were not excessive levels in frequency, they were natural and normal emissions impacting my emotions and physiology. Can you imagine, a person walking down the street, walking through a number of fields and their emotions changing almost as quickly?

When I didn't have the knowledge of how deeply sensitive I was (or empathic), I was constantly sent intellectually and emotionally off balance. I felt like an emotional rollercoaster, and those around me were on the ride too.

Kids & Their Environment:

After going to bed, my oldest son Jadon came out to the living room and told me that he felt like "someone" was under his bed. Because I was so looking forward to my "adult time", I took a deep breath to clear my head so I could begin productively troubleshooting with him.

(For those who are not trained in 'feeling' electromagnetic fields, there are EMF meters available for sale on the internet that can help you find higher concentration of these fields.)

We went into my son's room and I asked him where he felt that "someone" was.

He told me, "under his bed".

So I sat on his bed for a moment. Moved away; then sat back down. There was definitely a different feeling from one part of the room to the other.

I examined my feelings by moving back and forth, and realized that what he was experiencing were EMFs produced by the electrical outlet that his bed was pushed up against.

We moved his bed and he was able to fall asleep.

My son now has a knowledge of how electrical currents affect him. He no longer thinks that it has to be paranormal. He now has options for troubleshooting when he is feeling scared.

That "ghost" under my sons bed was an electromagnetic field. Nothing more.

I want to make this statement.

*I am **not** ruling out paranormal. I am showing that there is much more to consider. Things that can be explained and backed up with proof can help calm your youngsters mind.*

There are other things that impact us in different ways through merely being in the field of that "things'" frequency.

Have you ever experienced being with someone you didn't know and feeling calm and peaceful? Then sitting with a different person you don't know and feeling agitated and provoked?

Our field is interacting with the field of the other person.

What we experience triggers an emotional response (good, bad or indifferent). That person who you feel agitated or provoked with _may_ _not_ be a bad person… but they may not be a good fit for your life. So you gravitate to what makes you feel good.

So how can something we can't see have an impact on us physically and emotionally?

Think of air… we can't see it… but it is a most important element to keep us alive. How about gravity? We can't see it, but it's what keeps our feet on the ground.

Personally, I believe we are designed that way to help give us hints to follow our purpose, and lead us to those people and places that will help us grow and expand.

CHAPTER 5

Let's Break it Down –
What is Your Child Exposed To
and How is it Affecting Him?

- Emotional and Interpersonal Dynamics -

"Only by attaining knowledge
can one become…free from fear."
~ Rig Veda~

The next two chapters are to get you thinking about the possibilities of what could be disturbing your child. Here is a list of some emotional and interpersonal dynamics that may be affecting your little one:

- Attention Seeking
- Change in Routine
- Transference

Attention Seeking

Yep. That might be all it is. There are a couple of simple questions to ask yourself to get to the bottom of things:

» How much time are you spending with your child?

One of the most challenging thing as a parent is to give quality time to our kids. With families needing a double income to stay afloat, or the stresses of being a single parent, we find ourselves working for our family but never spending time with them. Is this familiar? Perhaps they are actively engaging you so you will spend more time with them.

My oldest son acts out in different ways when he needs time with daddy, than when he needs time with mommy.

However, my youngest is an equal opportunity terrorist, and uses the same attention getting techniques for both mommy and daddy.

» Does your child know how to "play" you?

As a parent, the first thing I would say is:

"NO! My child doesn't *"play"* me, thank you very much!"

But honestly, as Howard Glassner, author of *Transforming the Difficult Child,* would say, "You are your child's biggest toy."

Regardless of age, when your kid can see that certain behaviors result in attention from mommy and daddy (good or bad, right or wrong); they're going to try it out and continue to do it until it becomes an ingrained dynamic, unless the behavior is stopped by you, the parent. This is one way kids develop an understanding of their power.

Remember, your kids are going to try _____ (fill in the blank) out on YOU! I like to think of my kids as little explorers sailing in uncharted territories discovering things they love, like and dislike. Sometimes it doesn't feel like it, but it's our honor as parents for children to "try out" their behaviors on us. It's our gift and responsibility to teach them appropriate boundaries for themselves and the family as a whole through love, strength and consistency.

Discipline

Do you give in easily? Many times as parents our desire is to give our children everything that we didn't have growing up. In the process, boundaries can be blurred, and structures to help your child thrive are missed or not implemented.

Other times, we as parents feel 'guilt' for working too much, or focusing time on other obligations that take us away from spending time with our child.

Do you have guilt that is activated due to being a working parent, working toward goals that prevent you from more time with your child? Remember, your child benefits not only from your time together, the demonstration of responsibility and hard work are tremendously important for a child helping them understand work ethic and dedication.

The guilt can lead us to unclear boundaries and inappropriate behaviors (giving in) to compensate for lack of quality time.

So can sheer exhaustion.

If your working your tushy off at your job, and you want to just come home and relax… this is another time when we as parents "give in". Parental endurance is rarely talked about, and completely necessary to proactively work with our kids.

When I was working two jobs, and coming home to my oldest son (a three year old at the time), I did not have the endurance to keep up with his demands. I was exhausted. Thankfully my husband was there to pick up the slack.

I still have to be very conscious of what my children are asking me. I have to stay conscious that they do not assert their will over the rules of the house and that they are properly guided. A child having too much control or authority in the house, or too many choices, results in confusion and stress for not only your child, but for you as well. So parental endurance is a must.

Change in Routine

Have you experienced a change in routine, or living circumstances? Even something as simple as daylight savings, or relaxing bed time (getting the kids to bed later) can disrupt the evening harmony.

Is there a new sibling? Has your family gone through divorce? Have you moved, or experienced the death of someone close (or your family casually knows)?

Nero our beloved cat died at the end of summer. A couple of months later, our eighty year old neighbor passed away, and all that my youngest would talk about at bedtime was death (his "boogieman" of the moment).

- "When are we going to die?"
- "Where do you go when you die?"
- "Is there blood when you die?"

Almost a year later, it was still on his mind.

Here are some questions regarding changes in routine:

- Is your child a night owl or early bird? Has that changed?
- Will your child be starting school soon or changing care providers?
- Have you incorporated a new activity in your family's routine? (even fun changes can bring unexpected fear issues)
- Is your child's meal schedule erratic? Children can have stress when they forget to eat or have erratic diets.
- Have you moved?

- Have living arrangements changed? (i.e. new sibling, caring for an elderly relative, housing international students, remodeling the house)
- Does your child currently have behavior problems and did this start before or after issue with sleeping?
- What kind of discipline do you use?

Not every child is the same and discipline can (and sometimes should) be customized for each child. The main consistency should be just that... consistency. Whatever the action that is not in alignment with your family values must have a consequence. The "how's" can vary. (A common complaint with multiple children. Having different discipline styles for each child may not seem "fair".

(I don't know who got us to believe life was "fair" in the first place... but we all have our lessons to learn. My sister and brother got the skinny gene and I've always been larger. That didn't seem fair to me either. When my son expresses his frustration with his brother not being disciplined "as much" as he is, I remind him of their age difference, and level of responsibilities are different. If that still doesn't help and he stomps his foot and says, "THAT'S NOT FAIR!" I say, "repeat after me... 'Life is not always fair, but I can handle it.'")

- Does your child play well on his own?
- Is your child more social, and require more interaction?

These are just some questions to explore. Your child is so unique, and there is no manual that will fix the "problem". You know your life best. What's changed? Even the most subtle things can, and sometimes do, make a difference.

Transference

What fears are your kids exposed to? Is dad freaked out about snakes? Or is mom strangely fascinated with sharks?

My family went camping through the Canadian Rockies one summer. We were in "full on" bear territory. Even though we live in the Pacific Northwest, at the time I wasn't well versed in bear activity. But it was time to get a crash course with two young boys to look after. The one thing I did know is that they came out to forage in the early morning, or around dusk.

It was the last day of our visit in the town of Revelstoke, a picturesque town nestled in the majestic beauty of the Rockies. We wanted to make the most of the remains of the day so we went to the visitor center for some tips. The wonderful ladies there all concurred that the place we could not miss was the look out at the top of Mt. Revelstoke.

Since it was our last day my husband said, "Let's drive to the top of the mountain".

My initial response was, "FUN! Let's do it!"

Then it started getting a little dark.

With every curve in the winding "Meadows in the Sky Parkway", I was CERTAIN we were going to run into a bear and it wouldn't be good. I didn't say a word other than, "I think it's getting too dark to really enjoy the lookout."

While I braced myself in my seat and remained very quiet up the winding mountain road, I was getting increasingly scared… not only for myself, but for my kids. And to my dismay, my oldest son started to say… "Daddy, I think mommy's right, we should turn around"…

We were perfectly safe in our car. My husband has had plenty of experience with being in bear country, but I was scared, and my fear transferred on to my son.

It put a damper on the whole experience because of my fears.

Turning the experience around...

I gathered and read a bunch of literature on what to do in case you encounter a bear, and shared it with my son. We didn't see any more bears for the duration of the trip, but two weeks later and 15 minutes from our home, I went hiking with my kids and friends. What happened? We spotted a black bear walking toward our trail. Because we knew what to do, Jadon and I were able to use the tools that we read about to encourage the bear to turn around... and sure enough, it did. My son was a true leader making noise and telling the other kids to get together.

It was exhilarating to share this experience with him, and to successfully work through both of our fears.

Can you think of a time that you or your partner unknowingly (or knowingly) transferred your fears on to your child?

The moment you recognize it, do your best to educate yourself and your child.

CHAPTER 6

Let's Break it Down –
What is Your Child Exposed To
and How is it Affecting Him?
- Environmental influences -

"Where I grew up - I grew up on the north side of Akron, lived in the projects.
So those scared and lonely nights - that's every night.
You hear a lot of police sirens, you hear a lot of gunfire.
Things that you don't want your kids to hear growing up."
~LeBron James~

We can provide the most loving and nurturing home for our kids, and there may be some things that slip by our detection that are impacting them at a subconscious level such as:

- EMFs
- Subliminal Stimuli
- Internalizing
- Paranormal Phenomenon

EMFs (electro-magnetic fields)

I spoke briefly about electromagnetic fields and how they can promote paranoia, headaches and even nausea in sensitive individuals. So here are a few things to investigate in your child's room and around your home.

» Is it an old house?

» Does the house have electrical issues?

» Are there power lines around the house?

» Are there streams under or around the house?

» Do you live in an earthquake area?

» Are you over a fault line? (Even minor ones?)

» What was the land use for before?

» Do utilities run under the house?

While investigating these things, check them specifically against where your child sleeps. I strongly suggest that if you yourself are not trained or used to using your empathic abilities, that you either:

1. Hire someone to come in and test your outlets.
   Or
2. Purchase an EMF meter. (The EMF meter will not help you find out about lay lines, fault lines or streams.)

Remember, even in what is considered "normal" ranges, they are impacting our field.

Subliminal Stimuli

Subliminal means "below threshold". Subliminal stimuli is when information is coming in to your awareness subconsciously. This information is being sorted and distributed in the best way that you understand and associate the information.

A study was conducted by Vaughn A. Kaser called *"The Effects of an Auditory Subliminal Message upon the Production of Images and Dreams"*, and published by the Journal of Nervous & Mental Disease. It stated "based on the statistical data and certain drawings collected in this study, it would appear that the auditory subliminal message did have an effect upon the imagery, and dreams of the subjects in the experimental group."

As I write this I am hearing multiple streams of subliminal stimuli…. police sirens, helicopters and traffic going by… as I become more aware of how my body reacts to the information (sounds), I realize that instinctively and immediately my body and subconscious are determining if I am in danger, and wonder who may be in danger. Although I'm safe and without concern for my wellbeing, the sounds trigger a feeling of slight instability and insecurity.

With this in mind, if your child can hear activity coming from another room, and can't quite make out what's being said or what's happening… but can hear a word or two periodically… well that is reaching your child's subconscious mind. Your voice… music…

television… etc. are being filtered into the mind at a perceptible level of awareness. The human subconscious is indiscriminate with the information it accepts over a lifetime.

Hearing a shoot'em up action movie can play havoc on a little one's subconscious mind, if they can hear gun fire and sirens. The quote from Lebron James really drives it home for me. He removed himself from an environment where there were *real* guns and violence, but our entertainment is to bring it into our homes.

How is your house configured? Where is your child's room? Can they hear movies, music, conversations or arguments from their bedroom??

Do an experiment. At night, engage in any normal activity to see if the noise reaches your child's room. Quietly go into your child's room and see if the sound travels.

It may sound far-fetched… but I remember the first time I was aware that a song filtered into my dream time. I was in high school and I would be awakened by my radio alarm clock. I was dreaming that I was skipping down the halls of my school. The walls were stark white and it was dimly lit. I was dressed in white clothes with a straight jacket singing "they're going to take me away to the funny farm". I woke up abruptly and I heard the tail end of that same song playing on my radio.

Even sounds of sexuality can be a confusing and possibly disturbing sound for your child. Are you vocal in your lovemaking? This can seep into your child's subconscious. They don't have a framework for that information, and may put it into context of someone being hurt, or the moans of a "monster".

Internalizing

Is your child taking on information that they are hearing, seeing or engaged with?

Let me give you an example:

My son Jadon started having night terrors. When we asked him what he was feeling or seeing, he stated that there were a bunch of red dots closing in on him. He was for some reason afraid of the red dots.

His night terrors were getting worse and worse.

Now since my husband and I work together, it seems like most of our conversation revolves around business, our websites, gaining a competitive edge in our marketing and advertising... what we discovered is our animated conversations around the dinner table were the same topic... dot com this, dot com that.... www dot whatever dot com.

Jadon was internalizing our conversations... come to find, our animated conversations were causing him stress. Although my husband and I wouldn't consider the conversation stressful, our son did. Those red dots that were terrorizing him were a direct influence from our dinner conversations.

When we uncovered the source of his night terrors and helped him release his anxiety, his night terrors went away completely.

This dovetails with the subliminal stimuli. Although my son was not an active part of the conversation, he was internalizing the content.

Another way our kids internalize is with peer play. What is your kiddo playing at recess or talking about with his friends? I have observed my son and other children becoming very sensitive when they are playing "tag". Initially, there is the joy and fun of not getting "tagged". But when the chase goes on a little longer, suddenly you see a shift in the child's face to a slight panic. I've seen children start crying in the middle of the run on both ends. The one feeling chased may start to feel like prey. The one chasing can begin to feel left behind. I've seen groups of two, three and four year olds play the "monster" game where one of the children pretend to be a monster and is going to "get" the other children. Another game is called "warrior" with children chasing imaginary monsters and witches. All of these games, even "tag", can evoke fears within the chase. I'm not saying the kids should stop playing these games… I'm saying they can have an impact on bringing up fears.

Paranormal

Although paranormal is my main focus in my daily practice, it is the last thing I suggest considering as it is the most challenging to prove or explain. Plus there are so many religious beliefs that shun dialogue on the matter, and scientific naysayers that simply believe due to "scientific deduction" it is not possible. But something is going on that can't be explained, and it can't be *completely* disproven either.

With that said, if you are not familiar in working with these paranormal energies, I strongly suggest you find someone who is. Trying to "handle" the paranormal on your own without appropriate guidance is inadvisable.

For those of you who feel that your child is dealing with paranormal activity, the best resources to help you understand energy and give detailed information on clearing unwanted energies would be *The Moment that Matters: Restore balance to your home, your life and your environment through awareness and responsibility…* by Eric Dowsett and *Space Clearing A-Z; Space Clearing; Sacred Spaces: Clearing and Enhancing the Energy of Your Home* all by Denise Linn. Some of the exercises to do with your child in Chapter 11 can help ameliorate these issues as well.

If you're not comfortable with investigating and clearing and it doesn't match your belief structure, the best point of reference and assistance is to contact your local church, a reputable Feng Shui expert, or local metaphysical bookstore for direction and guidance.

Although the paranormal and esoteric have been my focus, over the years I have found it equally important to thoroughly consider the all other possibilities, as there are so many variables to our kiddo's journey.

CHAPTER 7

Is there Something More to Consider?

"All that is valuable in human society depends upon the opportunity for development accorded the individual."
~Albert Einstein~

Developmentally we go through various "fear triggers"... fear of strangers... fear of loud noises... fear of animals, masks, doctors *and* the boogieman. If those fears aren't addressed and understood, they can evolve to added unnecessary fears and neurosis. Such as fear of loss, fear of intimacy, fear of change.

Some of us are hardwired for certain restrictive and introverted behaviors, and others for more permissive and extroverted behaviors. It's up to us to navigate and guide our children based on our gut/feelings and who these little people show us they are.

By now, I'm sure you've read a number of articles and books on child development, and have realized that children have their own unique physical and emotional development markers. Yet each child is different and develops in their own way and in their own time.

In 1956 psychiatrist Erik Erikson conducted extensive research of children and their development stages in cross socio-economical households. What came of that study was what he called "Eight Stages of Pyschosocial Development".

Age	Conflict	Resolution or "Virtue"	Culmination in old age
Infancy (0 -1 year)	Learning Basic Trust vs. Basic Mistrust	Hope	Appreciation of interdependence & relatedness
Early Childhood (1 – 3 years)	Learning Autonomy vs. Shame	Will	Acceptance of the cycle of life
Play age (3 – 6 years)	Learning Initiative vs. Guilt	Purpose	Humor, empathy, resilience
School age (6 – 12 years)	Industry vs. Inferiority	Competence	Humility, acceptance of the course of one's life
Adolescence (12 – 19 years)	Learning Identity vs. Identity Diffusion	Fidelity	Sense of complexity of life; merging of sensory, logic & aesthetic perception
Early adulthood (20 – 25 years)	Learning Intimacy vs. Isolation	Love	Sense of the complexity of relationships; value of tenderness and loving freely
Adulthood (26 – 64 years)	Generativity vs. stagnation	Care	Caring for other, empathy and concern.
Old Age (65 – death)	Integrity vs. Despair	Wisdom	Existential identity; a sense of integrity strong enough to withstand physical disintegration.

Since Dr. Erikson's work, our world has changed significantly. I see how children are forced to cope with most all of the items on the conflict list by at least 10 years old or earlier. We, as parents and caregivers, are dealt a hand that forces us to broach topics that our parents either waited till we were older, or just never spoke to us about them at all. Our kids are being bombarded with things that scare me as a parent such as drugs in our elementary schools, sexuality in our middle schools, violence and bullying over all; not to mention, natural disasters, our country at war, terrorism.

It's not a conversation of "don't take candy from strangers" anymore. There are some real hard hitting conversations that we're having with the five plus kids. And if you're not talking about it at home, the kids are at school. Be sure that they are going to hear about it from their classmates.

Our kids are growing up fast. There is a quote from the movie West Side Story that sticks in my head that I feel really epitomizes each generation. When Action said *"When 'you' was my age? When my old man was my age, when my brother was my age... You was never my age, none of ya!"*

We never have been the age of our children. They are exposed to things we never were because it simply didn't exist.

My mother sometimes still gets mad at me when I won't feed my children things that she fed us as kids. She would say, "well it was good enough for you! And I ate it when I was a kid."

When I was a kid, and when my mother was a kid, our food had more nutrient value. Now our food is processed, double processed with chemicals and hormones. Our food is killing us, and it's showing up not only with potential weight issues, but our children's behavior too.

Nutrient Deficiencies

Serveral times we had the pleasure of interviewing Dr. Billie Sahley, a Board Certified Medial Psychotherapist, Psychodiagnostician, Behavior Therapist & Orthomolecular Therapist. Dr. Sahley used her expertise in the field of orthomolecular medicine (science of the right nutritional molecules in the right amount) to assist individuals with chronic issues such as anxiety, fear, stress and pain.

One thing that Dr. Sahley explains is that the mother can only pass on genetically the same amount of neurotransmitters to their babies as they have themselves. Therefore, if the mother's serotonin levels are low, then the child's serotonin levels will be low too. The doctor goes on to say that due to the nutrient depletion in our diets, children and adults are not getting the proper nutritional building blocks for healthy brain function.

Children who are exhibiting anxiety and fear may be out of balance in their brains nutrients and require an amino acid panel to determine healthy levels.

There are noninvasive tests that can be performed in determining if your child is lacking proper amino acids, vitamins and mineral nutrients. All of these things can be bring on physiological symptoms that induce stress and anxiety.

Allergies

Is your child eating before bed?

Allergies are another reason for children to act out and cause emotional stress.

Multiple studies have been done showing that certain artificial food dyes made from petroleum would frequently cause children to act erratically. Processed wheat, corn and milk are known to be big offenders causing kids to have chronic sleeping problems, and those are all huge staples in the average American diet. For a more in-depth look at nutrition and allergies, check out *Is This Your Child?* by Doris Rapp, M.D.

Head Trauma

Dr. Daniel Amen is a psychiatrist, brain specialist, author and medical director of the Amen Clinic. He has done extensive researchers on brain activity. He is finding solutions for those who suffer varying brain functions.

In researching his material *Healing ADD Breakthrough Program that Allows you to Heal 6 Types of ADD*, although all of the ADD profiles present their own unique issues that encourage stress and anxiety, there was one type that stood out to me: Type 4: Temporal Lobe ADD.

Dr. Amen states that the core symptoms of Type 4 are:

- History of a head injury or family history of violence or explosiveness
- Imagines visual changes, such as seeing shadows or objects changing shape
- Has periods of panic and/or fear for no specific reason
- Has a tendency to become increasingly irritable, then explode, then recede, and is often tired after a rage.
- Has periods of spaciness or confusion
- Has periods of quick temper or rages with little provocation
- Frequent periods of déjà vu
- Is sensitive or mildly paranoid
- Experiences headaches or abdominal pain of uncertain origin.

Has your child had a head trauma (even a slight one such as falling off a swing or whiplash from a fall)?

CHAPTER 8

Nurturing Your Child's Emotional Intelligence

*"Emotional Intelligence is a way of recognizing, understanding,
and choosing how we think, feel, and act. It shapes our interactions
with others and our understanding of ourselves.
It defines how and what we learn; it allows us to set priorities;
it determines the majority of our daily actions.
Research suggests it is responsible for as much as 80%
of the 'success' in our lives."*

~

Who are the most successful people in business? People who trust their "gut"... and follow it.

What does this have to do with anything and why do we care?

We all want our children to be successful. So how do we do that?

We help them understand their emotional landscape (fear, joy, suspicion, insecurity, etc.) to enable them to "trust their gut".
We are taught from the moment we leave the womb to trust someone else to care for us, and meet our needs... food, clothing, shelter,

education, love.   The one thing that is unintentionally missed… is learning self-trust.

I know… it comes with age and experience… well, not necessarily. I know a lot of men and women well into their 40's, 50's and 60's who don't know how to trust themselves.

So what does this have to do with helping your child work through night time fears?

Quite a bit actually.

Whether you think your child is highly empathic or not, it is vital to teach them about their emotions, and how to effectively trust and share their feelings. I have found that if your child has an abundance of unexpressed feeling this too may impact their ability to sleep.

Like most people my age, I grew up in a time when children were to be seen not heard. And if you did see them or hear them, they were to be pleasant and happy. Sure we could fall down, cry and be sad or scared for a minute, but to show anger or resentment (my father liked to call that "silent insolence") was intolerable.

Times have changed and it's no longer blasphemous to speak your feelings. Thankfully it's now encouraged. We still need to teach our kids how to behave in public, and how to put their best foot forward.

But now, if we're feeling hurt, upset or disappointed, it's okay to share those emotions too.

It's imperative that we teach our children how to effectively communicate their emotions, and "use their words" at every available opportunity. Assisting your child in understanding their emotional landscape in a simple way gives them the foundation and solid starting point for self knowledge and self trust.

Here are a couple of examples of how too much on our kids' mind can bring up anxiety, tension and stress:

Phoenix

I was putting my 3 year old Phoenix down for bedtime; he was cranky and fussy then started to pretend fight with "bad guys" and talking about "killing the monsters".

When the lights were out he said to me, "Mommy, when Henry died there was lots of blood."

I said to him, "No honey, there wasn't any blood. Henry died because his body was old and God wanted him to come home."

Phoenix responded, "Oh. Was there a lot of blood when Nero died?"

I told him, "No honey, Nero was old. And when we get really old and have done everything we're here to do, then we die. But that doesn't happen until we're really, really old. And only God can say when it's time for us to die."

Use whatever your belief structures are… but if your kid is talking about a certain topic, they are not too young to have an age appropriate modified conversation to help ease their concerns.

Paula

Sarah was putting 8 year old Paula to bed. Paula was being resistant, crying and giving excuses why she should stay up. Paula listed everything from being hungry to being scared. Sarah knew these where signs that Paula had a stressful day.

Sarah said to Paula, "Do you want to talk about your day?"

Paula stopped for a minute and took a deep breath and replied, "u'huh."

Sarah said, "Okay, then let's talk while you're lying down and cozy."

Paula laid down and started sharing her day with her mom. Come to find, she was holding on to a situation that happened at school which hurt her feelings and made her feel insecure.

As Paula shared her feelings with her mom, Sarah sat and listened asking her questions, helping Paula identify her feelings. Once Paula's feelings were acknowledged, she began yawning. Her mother took that as the cue to wrap up the conversation and Paula went to sleep.

After a long day, do you feel the need to talk with your partner or friend about what happened, helping you decompress and acknowledge the stresses of the day? Before you go to bed, do you enjoy a little talk with your partner to relax and connect?

Our kids are no different. Many times I'm in such a hurry to put my kids to bed so I can have "my time" to connect with my husband that I sometimes forget that my kids need that as well.

It's important that if your child is dealing with fear at night or resistance to sleeping that taking time to talk about their day in their room, making the environment cozy and nurturing, that they will naturally start seeing their bed and room as a safe and welcoming place to be.

It's important to remember that teaching our children to understand their emotions means we, as parents and care providers, need to understand ours. So one of the best way for us to assist our children with understanding their emotions is to use our emotional words too.

Many parents feel that showing vulnerable emotions to their children may place the parent/child dynamic off kilter. So as parents, we tend to lump most of our feeling in with "happy", "angry", "sad" and "scared". There are a myriad of emotions that need and deserve their own identity providing not only our children with the sound emotional modeling, but also encouraging the family to understand their rich emotional identity.

Also, our kids are inadvertently tuning in to our tensions (which is a stress for them as well). And to acknowledge our stresses and frustrations validates what they are already feeling. *Which helps them trust their feelings.* There are ways to share your vulnerable emotions without being inappropriate or over sharing, giving up your place of authority.

Has your child ever asked you if you're "mad" at them when really you've just had a tough day?

When my kids ask me that question I really pause and check in with myself before I give them my answer which can be a variety of things such as:

- "No honey, I'm not mad at you. I've had a bit of a frustrating day. But it's nothing you need to worry about."

This type of a response validates that their feelings were accurate, building their self-trust. This type of response will *also* help them to not misinterpret who or what your feelings are aimed toward, and gives them peace of mind to know that they needn't worry. Again, this directly helps them develop trusting their gut.

Maybe you *are* upset with their behavior, but you may not be "mad".

- "I'm not mad at you, but I am disappointed with your behavior."

Again, you are validating their feelings and helping them expand their emotional vocabulary.

Has your child ever told you they "hated" you? If so, how did you handle it? Did you provide a space for their feelings, or did you tell them to "never say that again" or did you collapse to their will?

When you give your child (or anyone for that matter) the space and permission to feel their feelings without taking it personally, it helps them process their feelings more quickly.

Mary Sheedy Kurcinka, author of *"Sleepless in America"*, gives a comprehensive look at American culture, and sleep issues. She states in her book, "When children are distressed, you cannot threaten, force, or beg them out of it. You have to address the feeling."

How can you do that?

By helping them know their feelings.

Every now and again we play a game with my kids called "who's the most…" We sit down and have the kids tell us between Mommy and Daddy who they think is:

- » "The most happy?"
- » "Gets mad the most?"
- » "Stays mad the longest?"
- » "Watches TV more."
- » "Plays the most."
- » "Who's smarter – braver – stronger?"

You get the picture. My husband and I have to be in a neutral place to make sure we aren't reactionary to their answers. This game helps our kids feel more comfortable that they can trust telling us their feelings, and it helps us know how they perceive us in a fun and playful way.

The last thing we want to do is teach our kids the landscape of their emotional world then turn around and discount their feelings. This leads to not trusting you, the parent, but also resentment, repression, guilt and shame. On the same coin, we don't let them override the structure of the family.

It may not seem like it... but this does tie in to sleep disturbances. Unexpressed feelings can wreak havoc on our psyche causing us to conjure up all sorts of things that bring us fear.

If your child needs to have a little extra time before bed to talk about their feelings from the day, take that time. Ask your child, "How do you feel?" (and don't settle for "good" or "I don't know" as their answer)... help them identify what they are feeling and experiencing. It makes a difference on so many levels. Not only in having a more restful sleep, but also helping you connect on a deeper level with your kids.

Great "feeling" words to use with your kids

- angry
- anxious
- bothered
- disappointed
- embarrassed
- frustrated
- lonely
- nervous
- rude
- sad
- uncomfortable
- unsure
- upset

- appreciate
- calm
- confident
- excited
- friendly
- grateful
- happy
- kind
- positive
- relaxed
- sensitive
- understand(ing)

The BEST words to use with your kids

- Love
- Forgive

CHAPTER 9

For Those of You with Teenagers

"This rite of passage taught me
that people are not always going to be there for me all my life.
I'm going to have to depend on myself to do things,
and believe in myself more."
~Maurice Tyson at age 13~

Although I have been focusing more on the three to ten year old range, the ideas in chapters 4, 5, 6, 7 and 8 apply to, and can be adapted for, your teenager.

At this age, most parents complain that they can't get their teenager out of their room, or they sleep too much. Teens need anywhere from 8 ½ to more than 9 hours of sleep per night. And if your teen is highly sensitive, they may require even more!

As your child develops, night terrors diminish, and should, as developmentally your teenager has the ability to analyze their own feelings and make decision based on knowledge of options and consequences.

Because their physical bodies are attaining full adulthood, and their emotions and intellect are not yet matching their new physical identity, these kids are running as fast as they can to catch up with becoming more independent, responsible and self-sufficient. As joyful as we are to see our children develop, it can be a scary time for everyone concerned.

This is such a sensitive age segment. Although our natural course of action is to give them more freedom, we still want to observe our kids carefully for any signs of depression, stress, fear and anxiety that prevent them from getting the sleep they require.

I want to state that there are times that troubleshooting on your own is not the best course of action, and that it may be necessary to consult your physician. The older our teen gets, more possibilities arise as to the cause of night terrors such as:

- Sleep disorders
  (sleep deprivation, obstructive sleep apnea, etc.)
- Medical Conditions
  (hyperthyroidism, migraine headaches, head injury, etc.)
- Lifestyle issues
  (a full academic and/or sports schedule, parental discord, sibling issues, peer pressure, loss of family or friend, etc.)

Medscape Education posted a study conducted by Kiki Chang, M.D. and Kim Galelli, Ph.D. on *Early Detection of Bipolar Disorder*. It was a retrospective study of adults with Bipolar Disorders that helped provide insight into the early expression of BD. They found that up to 65% of adults with BD had an initial mood episode *before* the age of 18 years. They have also linked a small percentage of children with ADHD to Bipolar Disorders.

These are things to take into consideration with episodes of fear, and night time issues in teens. Keep observing and asking your teen questions. Reading a book isn't going to change anything... taking time to troubleshoot with your child will.

Now let's go back to the basics...

Here are some things that may be attributed to your teens sleep issues:

Environmental / Technology

Whether we like it or not, our teens have more exposure to electromagnetic fields. As our kids get older and aren't with us all the time, cell phones are the best way to keep an eye on our kids. So now, there are a bunch of kids running around with cell phones in their pockets, backpacks and purses calling and texting you as well as their friends.

With cell towers practically on every corner, power lines and transformers over head and underground, we are all being bombarded all the time. (By the way... even cordless landline telephones have been documented to emit even higher EMF levels than cell phones).

Schools have computer labs. Libraries now offer free computer access. And, most homes have one or more computers, and kids are getting their own notebooks and laptops. Not to mention smartphones, handheld gamer devices with wifi capabilities and increased television usage.

Radio waves and microwaves all have a stressful impact on our physical body, potentially leading to chronic stress burnout which can kill vital brain cells. With more frequent usage of these technologies our kids' systems are not only being overloaded, they are being stunted while they're still developing.

I'm not suggesting throwing out technology, but there is a balance to establish for your family.

Read chapter 4 again (or if you haven't already – read it now.)

Gaining Independence

Having those heart to heart discussions with our teens can be a little more challenging as they begin to assert their independence, and gain more life experiences that don't involve us.

But it's not too late to encourage and foster a strong open dialogue with your teen. Encourage them to develop their emotional awareness, and impart tools that will assist them in their life to reduce stress, anxiety and fear.

If they are not used to emotional dialogue with you, they may try any tactic... from shutting down, to sarcasm, to full on condescending retort to avoid the conversation. Stay committed, consistent and most of all sincere. Teens can smell parental BS a mile away. Just look at it as planting seed.

It does and will pay off.

Diet

I touched on this in chapter 7 discussing nutrient deficiencies and allergies.

Food allergies can alter how you feel, act, behave, walk, talk, think and sleep. It's amazing to me that dyes and synthetic foams are allowed in our food!

I recently read an article that one of the most popular fast food restaurants out there actually has dimethylpolysiloxane which is made of silicone and is added as an "antifoaming agent". This is placed in the most commonly ordered item for children on the menu... I'm referring to chicken shaped in the easy to hold "nugget" form... YUM... I want my child to make that their healthy choice! NOT!

I see so many teens making crazy food choices when their parents aren't "watching". The sugar and junk food set up a system for stress and anxiety.

Hormones & Brain Development

Okay.... Our teens are undergoing normal, yet radical, body changes. Their hormones are hard at work changing their bodies... not only are their sexual hormones working overtime, so are the amino building blocks that help keep healthy neurosynapse firing in the brain.

Dr. Billie Sahley noticed in her work, that teens had an inordinate amount of psychological and physiological stresses that they are dealing with during their metamorphosis. So she founded *TeenUSA* to assist teens and young adults with anger, moodiness, sleep disruptions and addictions during this time.

Per Dr. Sahley, "Researchers have documented that hormones do impact brain development of teens. Serotonin and dopamine are the master hormones that govern mood and create control in extreme situations. Estrogen and testosterone are believed to trigger genetically linked behavior.

The amygdala is the emotional center of the brain where everything is stored, especially negative emotions. The amygdala is also a control center for the mind and body, and can release feelings of anger, fear, panic."

Dr. Sahley also states, "Research demonstrates alterations of function in the limbic system causes changes in emotional responses as rage, fear, reasoning, and impulse control. The limbic system located deep in the brain's interior is associated with the roots of anxiety, panic, and fear. The limbic system stays in overdrive due to an excessive production of sex hormones. The teen years are a time of continuous changes in brain chemistry."

There is so much more going on than what meets the eye when our kids are developing.

School

With all the hormonal happenings, academic pressure combined with peer pressure can result in finding ways to cope with the stress. Many times teens turn to smoking, illegal drugs, prescription drugs and /or alcohol to fit in or "manage" their anxiety.

I've witnessed teens who have nightmares about upcoming tests, proms, overloaded schedules. With the new freedom of independence, some kids are making their own decisions to "self-medicate."

As we push our kids to become more independent, it is equally important that they know that we, as parents are here for them, giving them tools to reduce stress in a positive and healthy way.

Nothing is more valuable to your child then your continued guidance.

Note to Self: *(and all other parents)*
"Love does not mean a car at 16, or a trip to Cancun for spring break with their friends. Love is time, attention and direction."

Physical Exertion

A lot of parents do all they can to help a child find their physical and creative niche. For some, like my son, it's sports. Jadon enjoys art, choir, computers... but he *loves* physical activity.

We've discovered he is quite adept at downhill skiing, baseball, hockey and rollerblading. During ski season he had one day of ski school and one day of baseball clinics back to back. To us as parents, that didin't sound like too much. He was ecstatic to be doing both. But half way through his baseball clinic, his system was dehydrating quickly, and he would start to get mild migraine headaches.

We also noticed that during this time his sleep patterns changed, and his emotional sensitivity levels were heightened. The two days of intense physical exertion were not appropriate for his constitution. He required more rest time between the two sports. Or to choose another sport that didn't require as much physical exertion.

So many times we feel "busier is better", when it's really quality not quantity that truly enriches our kids.

Another thing to consider is sports injuries, specifically head injuries.
Dr. Daniel Amen author of *Healing Anxiety and Depression* speaks about head injures quite a bit and how that can impact behavior.

In Dr. Amen's book *Healing ADD Breakthrough Program that Allows you to Heal 6 Types of ADD*, the core symptoms of the one he has labeled "Temporal Lobe ADD" can stem from head injury.

Here are some of the symptoms

- Spaciness
- Confusion
- Panic and/or fear for no specific reason
- Visual changes (i.e. seeing shadows or objects changing)
- Illusions

- Sensitive or mildly paranoid.

Any of the above can trigger nighttime (or daytime) fears making it challenging to cope. To learn more I would recommend reading his book for extended details on cause and treatments if you feel your child may fall into this category.

Paranormal

Dr. Amen's work directly bleeds into the subject of paranormal.

Taking his type 4 ADD profile into consideration, there may be times when we "think" something paranormal is happening when in fact it's not. So discerning between physiological imbalances and paranormal activity is a must when considering all things.

I say this with the utmost authority.

When I was four years old, an embarrassing little accident occurred. I was visiting our pony Misty in our field. When I walked behind her, she was spooked and bucked, kicking me squarely in the head. Less than a year after that occurrence, I started seeing "shadows", and became increasingly paranoid that I was being watched. Thankfully, my mother left the dialogue open for anything.

My entire life I believed what I was seeing was paranormal and it may very well was...

BUT, when I discovered the *possibility* that it might NOT be paranormal, I had to scour my beliefs to help me see what was real and what was not real.

During that time of self-examination, I clearly remembered my very first paranormal experience was well BEFORE "the kick". So in my case, paranormal AND head injury may be both at work.

Regardless, teenagers are highly susceptible to the influence of unseen energies.

When I was old enough to start researching on the paranormal, the resources available to the public were limited. And as a teenager, you are exposed to strong influences that attempt to sway you in both directions of what I loosely call "positive" and "negative" energy. It's a time when teenagers are experimenting with who they want to be as independent adults. So they are more vulnerable to the influence of energies around them.

Some things to Consider:
- Is your teen choosing friends that are exposing him/her to negative experiences?
- Is your teen showing interest in the occult?
- Is your teen showing interest in religious or spiritual pursuits beyond the typical paranormal movie of the moment??

If your family does not have a spiritual or religious practice helping anchor your child to a positive path, it may make life more challenging when "negative" energies come in to their field.

The one thing that our children are missing in our culture is a rite of passage as a transitioning marker into adulthood connecting them to their purpose.

If your teen is dealing with energies from the other side… it is imperative that they understand the power in which they were given as a birthright from God.

The truth is that NOTHING can harm you unless you give it permission.

Allison

Paranormal Energy Clearing & Evolutionary Beliefs

I received an email from a dear friend explaining that her fifteen year old daughter was awakened by a dark mass hovering over her.

Her daughter had spent the night in her living room, and would not go back to her bedroom.

This family is not overtly religious, and does not have a daily spiritual practice per se, but they are very spiritually conscious, and openly and respectfully banter about their beliefs. The daughter has more of an evolutionary concept of the spiritual, leaning into the idea of nature and it's elements.

I immediately sent them a clearing protocol that engaged their unique beliefs, combined with claiming their God given energetic rights.

Within an hour of coming together as a family, invoking the pure love of God, the energy was gone.

To me, this clearly shows how not understanding our personal power can result in malicious energetic activity.

The heavy and negative energies FEED off of fear. The biggest illusion that we live is that we have no power. That belief is a breeding ground for negative paranormal experiences.

CHAPTER 10

Working out the Stress
and Standing up to Fear

"While we try to teach our children all about life,
our children teach us what life is all about."
~ Angela Schwindt~

We, as parents, are our children's first defense toward reducing or minimizing fear and stress, as well as understanding the world. We can also be the first person to activate those fears and stresses too.

My kids show me everyday who I am in the way they get angry, show affection, play, work, avoid, etc. Sometimes I feel amazed witnessing the positive impacts I have on them. And sometimes I cringe when I see the negative ones.

I firmly believe that no matter how hard we try to be good parents, we still wind up as fodder for the therapy couch. All of us require our challenges to help us develop into the individuals we are meant to be.
For me fear has been a lifetime lesson. Standing up to fear whether it's speaking my mind, finishing a project or making decision that impacts more than just myself.

If we start early enough to help our kids now, they will be far ahead of the curve in the theater of life. My hope is that this book, particularly this chapter, will give you and your child tools to build confidence and security, making fear a tool for navigating live vs. fear as a way of living life.

If you jumped directly to this chapter, I encourage you to reference back to previous chapters to help understand the reference points for these exercises.

NOTE:

In our home, we take a God and prayer focused approach. Many of the tools provided in this chapter are based in our beliefs. Please note, regardless of your spiritual and/or religious beliefs, the tools outlined in this book can be adapted to suit your life, lifestyle, belief structures without dishonoring or invalidating your beliefs. In fact I've been delighted in seeing how people of all different walks of life find that these tools actually enhance and honor their values.

The practices in this chapter are useful to adults as well. Take a look at what scares YOU and work with it. Look it in the face and know that you are positive and powerful. God has made us this way. There is no need for apology or approval to stand in this knowing. This (from my perspective) is who God wants us to be.

List of Exercises

1. Active Imagination
2. Affirmations

3. Aromatherapy

4. Breathing Exercises

5. Electromagnetic Protection

6. Energy Clearing of Paranormal or Negative Activity

7. Games

8. "In the Dark" Exercises

9. Muscle Testing

10. Prayers

11. Quiet Time / Meditation

12. Reading

13. Rituals

14. Subliminal Recordings

15. The "Why" Game

Exercises 0 – 36 Months (in utero as well!)

See Exercise: 1, 3, 5, 6, 8, 10, 11, 12, 13, 14

You will need to do most of the work, but it is anchoring tools they may need as they get older.

Exercises 2 ½ years and beyond

All the exercises are appropriate for any age group over 2 1/2 . Remember the younger they are the more direction they will need. Be sure to make it fun for them. Older kids can be empowered to do this on their own… but there is such a beautiful bonding that happens when the family comes together and shares in the experience.

In Alphabetical Order

1. Active Imagination

» **Children Under 6:** Does your child have a wonderful, yet active imagination? Then there is a sleep aid specifically designed for children to have a more sound sleep. (i.e. Hyland 4kids Calms Forte) This over-the-counter homeopathic is designed to safely and effectively counteract mental and physical restlessness in children. Studies show that 69% of our children under 10 years of age are prone to some kind of sleep problem. Calms Forté 4 Kids™ is a formulation of all natural, safe and effective ingredients. (no I don't get a kickback for suggesting this product!) – Remember, always check with your doctor first.

» **Children over 6:** Set aside some quiet time to just sit and talk. Talk about the day. Ask them questions about what they've already told you. Ask them about their friends and how they're doing. Show interest in the nuances of their day away from you. This will help them unload what's on their mind and keep you involved in their experiences.

You can also listen to soft melodic music or read with/to them. Choose stories that have a positive message… keep it light.
Family "after dinner" walks can be amazing. Our youngest and oldest take the hills with us and when it's time for bed, they're both worn-out and fast asleep within minutes.

Regarding nutrition and active imagination, remember, allergies don't just show up as skin irritations. It shows up in over active imaginings and behavior. So nutrition and brain function are imperative in considering what's going on for your child. Over active brain function may be a result of allergies to certain foods or dyes, poor nutrition.

Track what your child is consuming during the day… how much processed foods, additives, preservatives, sugar and sugar substitutes are they ingesting? With potential food allergies, I would suggest seeking out a Nutritionist or Naturopathic Physician to help pinpoint possible allergies.

2. **Affirmations** (any time of day)

My name is: _____, God has made me strong and nothing can harm me. I'm here to do great things, and to work with God. *(Modify this to fit your specific religious/spiritual/non-spiritual belief system… for Atheists. Take "God" out all together and use your value system.)*

I would use this when my son would wake up from night terrors. It helps them return to a state of personal power.

3. **Aromatherapy**

Essential oils have been used for centuries in relaxation. The most well know are:

- Lavender
- Chamomile

There are electric diffusers that you can purchase so you do not have to leave a candle burning in your child's room. Safety first!

Start the diffuser about a half hour or hour before bedtime, and keep the house as quiet as possible. This will help your child (and you too) release tensions, and unwind from the day.

When using aromatherapy, be sure to use only pure essential oils. Oils that are not pure may contain synthetic chemicals that will do more harm than good. See a good resource for pure oils in the back of this book.

4. Breathing Exercise

➤ **Power Breath** – Have your child sit however they are comfortable and close their eyes and take five deep belly breaths in through the nose and out the mouth. Then have your child imagine warmth and unconditional love in their heart. "cuddly" and "fluffy" are two great words to help them understand. Have them imagine that it is glowing any color they want. When that glow goes beyond their heart and fills their chest, arms, head, stomach, legs and feet, then have them extend that glow beyond their body, until they are surrounded by a big bubble. Once they feel the bubble around them, have them squeeze their hand to remember how safe and loving the bubble feels. Any time they need to feel safe, they need only to squeeze their hand to remember they are protected.

5. Electromagnetic Protection

➤ **Dowse Your House** – Use an EMF Meter or find a professional dowser to find the lay lines, fault line, etc. that could be impacting your child. *See Resources for Clearing/Dowsing.*

➤ **EMF Protection Devices** – If you suspect or have had a professional establish there are EMF frequencies in the home, use EMF disks to stop excessive EMF flow into the rooms that are being impacted. *See Resources for EMF Protection Devices.*

➤ **Furniture Placement** - Rearrange the furniture, make sure the bed is AWAY from electrical outlets. The older the house, the higher the possibilities of EMF interference.

6. Energy Clearing of Paranormal or Negative Activity

As with any energy clearing, it is vital that you and your child approach this with an open and pure heart. Below are some clearing rituals that you can do together. If you are not comfortable with this due to religious beliefs, contact the leader of your church and have them help you through prayer.

➤ **Clearing Statements** – Dear God, please remove any negative or dark energy from my personal field, room and home, and only allow the true essence of unconditional love.

➤ **Dowse Your House** – any spiritual dowser will not only be able to detect EMF misalignments….but they will also be able to detect if there are any lingering energies in your space. Perhaps there is discord in the house, wayward souls looking for the light or souls that have been on the land before mass population. Someone trained in this art will be able to give you feedback on the possibilities of these energies in your home.

➤ **Protection Bubble** – Have your child sit however they are comfortable and close their eyes. Have them imagine warmth and unconditional love in their heart. Have them imagine that it is glowing any color they want. When that glow goes beyond their heart and fills their chest, arms, head, stomach, legs and feet, then have them extend that glow beyond their body until they are surrounded by a big bubble. Once they feel the bubble around them, have them squeeze their hand to remember how safe and loving the bubble feels. Any time they need to feel safe, they need only to squeeze their hand to remember they are protected.

➤ **Prayer** – Whatever your religious or spiritual belief use, prayer from that source. We use the Catholic "Our Father". For those interested in that prayer here are the words:

> "Our Father, who art in Heaven, hallowed be Thy name. Thy kingdom come. Thy will be done on earth, as it is in Heaven. Give us this day our daily bread and forgive us our trespasses, as we forgive those who trespass against us. And lead us not into temptation and deliver us from all evil, for Thine is the Kingdom, the power and the glory forever and ever Amen".

Remember, use whatever feels right for you and your family.

➤ **Sage** – Sage has been used for centuries by indigenous people for blessings and clearings. This is called Smudging. You can also use essential oils in the same way to bypass setting off the smoke detectors in your home. Light the sage at one end, with pure intention, then start blowing throughout the space. It will begin to smoke a lot. While blowing this sacred smoke, use a prayer of your choosing. You can use the "Our Father," or Clearing Statement or whatever moves you. Have your child in on this, as they can be empowered to call on God whenever they need.

For more detail on energy clearing see the works of Denise Linn and Eric Dowsett. Their websites are listed in the Resources section of this book.

7. **Games**

➢ **Draw the Boogieman** – Have your little one draw a picture of his "monster". Name the monster and send him away. You can either burn the picture in the fireplace, bury it in the yard or tear it up. Dispose of it the way your child feels is best for him or her.

➢ **Monster Spray Away** – Our little ones are looking for ways to feel empowered, and this is a great tool. What you will need is a small spray bottle that is easy to pump, you fill with water and a special "monster be gone" elixir. I usually use lavender to help promote calming. When filling the pump you say a few magical words that bring in the feeling of protection. For example... With each drop of essential oil placed into the water, I usually say something like:

> "May all the monsters everywhere who come in this room be well aware that _____ (your child's name) has power indeed, and when he/she sprays you, you'll be history!"

Then have them spray all around the room.

This game is so much fun that it can get your kids wound up before bedtime. So be mindful when the spray comes out. Keep your kids calm. This was such a huge help for my son, Phoenix, that he only needed the feeling of security from the spray for about a month.

Then he forgot to ask for it night, after night and was able to get to sleep without issue.

➢ **Roughhousing** – Feeling comfortable in your body is highly important in feeling safe in the world. Controlled roughhousing is a deliberate way to help your child develop their physical identity, and recognizing how their body mechanics work, as well as neurologically releasing tensions. It's all about confidence building.

➢ **Room Search** – Look around the room together before going to bed… search the room for monsters. Let your child know that the reason monsters hide is because they're afraid of the child. This turns the tables from being a victim to one who's empowered. Remember… the monster may only be a metaphor for what the child is experiencing in his life. This is the outlet of subconscious fears.

If your child points to an imaginary (or real) "bad guy," have your child say "Go away. You are not allowed in my room. You cannot come back!"

8. Exercise

"In the Dark" Can we make darkness our friend, and be in the dark without fear? Absolutely. The darkness can be a wonderful place of exploration.

Sensory Games (using only sound, smell, touch & taste) help your child develop other senses.

When I'm with my kids outside at night, I deliberately talk to them about all the wonderful things that the night has to offer... the moon... the stars... all of the sounds that can be heard from crickets to the wind in the trees to small animals scurrying in the bushes.

You know your child best... use your imagination, and share with them all the things YOU like about the darkness. Have them tell you what they like back.

9. Muscle Testing

What Does Your Heart Say? – The phrase "Your Body Knows" is the key here. Sometimes our minds have a hard time "figuring out" what is for our highest and best good. But if we know how to quietly let our body tell us, we have an advantage.

First: Stand with your feet, shoulder width apart.

Second: Place your hands on your heart. Then remain quiet... think of the most quiet and peaceful thing you can... maybe it's God, maybe a meadow... whatever that thing is that brings you centered peace.

Third: Establish your body's "yes" and "no" answers. To do this, breathe deeply and ask your body to "show you" your "yes"... allow your body to tilt in the direction it naturally wants to go. Then ask your body to "show you" your "no". Allow your body to tilt in the direction it naturally wants to go. Once you can feel the difference between the two, your "yes" and "no" responses have been set.

Fourth: Ask your question…. (i.e. is this supplement right for me? Is my child's issue paranormal.? Is my child's issue related to the house's electrical frequencies? Is my child taking on to many activities? Is my child experiencing food allergies?)

Fifth: When you ask the question, allow your body to tilt. It will tilt in either your "yes" or "no" direction. This is how to get your "busy mind" out of the way and your subconscious "knowing" communicating with you.

You can teach this to your child when you feel that it is appropriate for them. My oldest son reminds me to do it when I'm struggling with a decision.

10. **Prayers** (before bed / before meals)

Add this to your nightly prayers…

My name is: _____ God has made me strong, and nothing can harm me. I'm here to do great things, and to work with God. *(Modify this to fit your specific religious/spiritual/non-spiritual belief system)*

11. **Quiet Time / Meditation**

➢ **Tree of Life** (Grounding): See your bare feet in the fresh moist healthy dirt… Feel the sensation of an endless stream of water running from the base of your spine down through your thighs… calves… ankles… and heels of your feet… streaming into the beautiful dark earth… down through the layers of dirt, clay, rock, sand and then rapping around the core of the earth… and coming back up through all of the rich, gorgeous layers... back up to the base of your feet... through your heels, ankles, calves, thighs and back up to the base of your spine making a connected loop securing you to the earth. Thank the earth for making this possible.

This can be used to release negativity. Send whatever sadness or negativity you've been feeling from the day/week/month/year and send it into the ground. Again, thank the earth for making that possible.

> **<u>Master in the Heart</u>** (Self-Nurturing): Visualize your chest... go deeper... go through the layers of your body, through your sternum... to your beautiful beating heart... healthy and pink... beating a strong heart song. Picture in your heart the teacher or ascended master that holds the most purity and meaning to you (examples: Jesus, Buddha, Krishna, Gandhi, Mother Teresa... etc.). See this master teacher as a baby curled in your heart... you are responsible for carrying this precious soul in your heart, and to ensure that he/she/it is cared for with deep unconditional love. This energy being inside of you radiates it's love and gratitude while you radiate love, peace and gratitude back. Let the feeling warm you throughout dissolving any discord you may be feeling.

(For very young children, use nature... maybe a flower blossoming. They are much faster at visualizing.)

12. **Reading** (especially for younger children)

There are wonderful books that help empower children, and recognize their innate strength, power and connection with all around. Please see some of my favorites listed in the Resource section of this book.

13. **Rituals**

➢ **Candle Ceremony** - Every night I have my boys set the intention for the evening and following day. While lighting a candle, they say: "My name is _____, and I light this candle in God's name to bring me _____" At the end, say a prayer and blow out the candle.

➢ **Empowerment Words** – Be sure to find reasons to show that you are proud of your child for their bravery and courage. Positive reinforcement encourages more of the same behavior.

➢ **Share Your Day** – unwind with a recap of your child's day. Who did they play with? How did they feel about the day? What did they like most? What did they like least? If they could change anything about the day, what would it be?

14. **Subliminal Music/Nature Sounds**

Use subliminal music in their room while they're sleeping. There are numerous CDs out there that promote healthy sleeping, and positive mental imaging that promote healthy self-esteem. Always be sure that the statements are calming and life affirming messages. Rotate them out.

See the Resource Section for my favorite websites.

15. The "Why" Game

This is by far one of my favorites! I see this not only as an exercise to help reduce fear, I use it as a catalyst to manifest what will assist in my personal growth. You can use this anytime for practically anything! This is a tool from Noah St.John called "AfFORMations." But for your kids' sake... it's "The WHY Game"! (Use this throughout the day.)

- "Why is it so easy to fall asleep?"
- "Why am I so safe?"
- "Why am I so smart?"
- "Why is school so fun?"
- "Why am I so happy?"
- "Why are people so supportive of me?"
- "Why am I so helpful?"

~~~~~~~~~~~~~~~~~~~~~~~~~~~~~~~~~~~~

Use any or all of this information as a metaphor... it still works.

Questions to Ask Yourself, and to Investigate:

- Is your child empathic? Chapter 3
- What is it to be an empath? Chapter 3
- Can your child hear your conversations from their room? Chapter 6
- Can your child hear music, or the television from their room? Are you watching violent shows, or having stressful conversations in their subliminal field? Chapter 6
- Has your child had a head trauma? Chapter 7
- Am I teaching my child to NOT trust themselves?

- "It's just your imagination."
- "Don't be silly."
- Am I teaching my child to have shame?
- "You big scaredy cat."
- "What's your problem?"
- Am I transferring my fears on to my child?
- "Heights freak me out."
- "I hate spiders!"
- Do I stick to my word? Can my child trust me? Broken promises = unable to trust the world.
- Do I say "No" with just cause, or because I don't want to be bothered? This could result in desires and vitality being diminished, or interpreted as not being valued and not worth the time (low self-worth).
- Am I SHOWING them how to move forward in spite of fear? Let them know something scares you, and show them you will do it anyway. Example: riding a bike / riding a horse / swimming – *disclaimer: always be sure it's age appropriate and truly safe to move forward.*

There are situations where I've caught myself saying or doing things for the sake of expedience that aren't in the highest and best interest of my children. But when we can catch ourselves… and take the time with your child to walk through the "not so scary" possibilities of why they're scared, you will be amazed at the results.

Most of all, be honest with your kids. They can already feel what's going on around them. Talk with them. *When they ask*, tell them you're sad, frustrated or angry, and reassure them that they are not the cause, and that it's temporary. This will ultimately help them trust you and themselves so much more.

Children's Books:

Because Nothing Looks Like God by Karen Kushner

Good Night Moon by Margaret Wise Brown

The Going to Bed Book by Sandra Boyton

I'm Not Afraid of You! by Lucia Davindia Steele

I Need My Monster by Amanda Noll

The Little Soul and the Son by Neale Donald Walsch

What is That? by Lucia Davindia Steele

Parent Aid Books:

Emotions

The Art of Roughhousing by Anthony DeBenedet & Larry Cohen

Building Emotional Intelligence by Daniel Goleman

The Highly Intuitive Child by Catherine Crawford

The Highly Sensitive Child by Elaine Aron

Sleepless in America by Mary Sheedy Kurchinka

Transforming the Difficult Child by Howard Glassner

Nutrition

Depression and more without Drugs – What to Use and When by Dr. Billie J. Sahley & Dr. Katherine M. Birkner

Fat, Sick & Nearly Dead (documentary) Director Joe Cross

Food Inc. (documentary) Director Robert Kenner

Food Matters (documentary) Director James Colquhoun, Laurentien Bosch

Heal with Amino Acids and Nutrients: Survive Stress/Anxiety, Pain,

Healing ADD: The Breakthrough Program That Allows You to See and Heal the 6 Types of ADD by Daniel G. Amen, M.D.

The Impossible Child: A Guide for Caring Teachers and Parents by Dr. Doris Rapp

Ingredients (documentary) Director Robert Bates

Is Ritalin Necessary? The Ritalin Report by Dr. Billie Sahley

Is This Your Child? Discovering and Treating Unrecognized Allergies in Children and Adults by Dr. Doris Rapp

Is This your Child's World? Is Your Child Allergic to Schools? by Dr. Doris Rapp

Stop ADD Naturally by Dr. Billie Sahley

Super Size Me (documentary) Director Morgan Spurlock

What's on Your Plate? (documentary) Director Catherine Gund

Clearing (Paranormal or Negative Activity)

The Moment that Matters by Eric Dowsett

Sacred Spaces by Denise Linn

Electromagnetic Fields

Electromagnetic Health: Making Sense of the Research and Practical Solutions for Electromagnet Fields (EMF) and Radio Frequencies by Casey Adams

Subliminal

Mind Programming by Eldon Taylor

Websites:

Behavior

www.EmpoweringParents.com

Brain Function, Nutrition Development

www.amenclinics.com

www.dorisrapp.com

www.painstresscenter.com

www.childdevelopmentinfo.com

Clearing/Dowsing (Paranormal or Negative Activity)

www.deniselinn.com

www.ericdowsett.com (Eric's site can direct you to Dowsers)

Communication

www.theboundariesmethod.com

EMF

www.earthcalm.com

Essential Oils

www.youngliving.com

Subliminal

www.innertalk.com

Skill Building Tools

www.theboundariesmethod.com

www.childhoodaffirmations.com

www.noahstjohn.com

TESTIMONIALS

"Moving to my new home was exciting, yet after meticulously cleaning and burning incense, I couldn't shake the feeling that the place needed a 'higher form of cleansing' that I wasn't educated enough to perform on my own. I wanted to be certain that I had chosen the right room to sleep in, the perfect room for creativity, and that things in the house were aligned for proper energy flow. Lucia's energy clearing work on my home made all the difference in getting rid of the residual energy from a long history of previous residents--clearing the canvas for a new picture. After the clearing, I could feel the air was lighter and something was definitely different. In addition to the home, we sat together and worked one-on-one to be certain I had detached from the old digs and fully rooted myself in the new environment. It was a fascinating process and I'm now insisting that other friends try doing the same to their homes--even if they haven't recently relocated."

*~ **T.A.** – Seattle, Washington*

~~~~~~

"Davindia is amazing. She is one of those rare people who constantly emanate an internal light of love, acceptance and grace. When my daughter was feeling a "presence" in her room, Davindia was able to prepare a guideline for a ritual my daughter could perform to remove this unwanted presence. She worked with my daughter and I and gave us both the confidence that we had the power to create the environment we wanted to create within our home and allow only positive and loving energy to remain. I call on Davindia whenever I feel a need for spiritual strength and guidance. Her incredible ability to connect with people, understand and empathize with their current situation and offer both comfort and guidance for personal empowerment and growth is second to none."

~**S. Burton**, mother of two ages 13 and 15.

ABOUT THE AUTHOR

Lucia Davindia Steele is a business woman, writer, humanitarian, systems implementor, mother and wife. For over a decade, Lucia Davindia, with her husband Cameron Steele, created and hosted an international internet program called Contact Talk Radio, interviewing pioneering speakers on cutting edge healing technologies and modalities, leading doctors, therapists, physicists and spiritual workers.

Contact Talk Radio is now an internet based radio station with dozens of hosts carrying on the legacy of connection, direction and meaning to its vast audience.

Lucia Davindia now divides her time overseeing the systems of the station, producing her writing projects, and her greatest achievement to date is being blessed with an amazing husband, their two sons and daughter.

Made in the USA
Lexington, KY
01 November 2015